Covert Psychology 101: The Great Leader Machiavelli Mindset Tactics Use To Access The Terrain Of Business For Pure Domination

By Calvin Kennedy

Table of Contents

INTRODUCTION

As human beings, we all strive to become the best that we can possibly become in life, often times when you ask people about their dreams; you tend to notice that human beings are limitless in their thinking. People in any field of life are often riddled with the easiest (or at the least, the least dreadful part) to the top; the reason for this isn't far-fetched, the view is better from the top. We are all born with the capability to dominate, the thing is that while some actualize their potentials by working towards it, others just let these potentials die in them. Another truth is that we cannot all be at the top, there needs to be some sort of separation or distinction between various groups of people. This is just the way the world was created, since this is the case, as humans we do the best that we can in order to get to the top (i.e. dominate).

There are various ways to arrive at the top, while some seem to be easier, others seem to be ruthless or evil. Either way, the way to the top is never an easy climb, this is true for every industry and every aspect of life. There are billions of people on earth today and it is only normal for people to have the same dreams as you for yourself or something that you are involved in. What then is the way out? How do we separate the boys from the men? Competition, war, or whatever you have to face in order for you to survive on your terms in the business world and in the world in general. Rivers, just like men are not to be trusted because both can be controlled when given power and intelligence and can become a force that can sweep the world away. There is always a new ground to be broken, a new achievement to get, a new role to assume therefore you must get into the now and find out what you must do to get the desired end. In life, more often than not, our actions are to be mainly influenced by the results of the actions taken, as it is what really matters. Being result oriented will not only help you stay focused but also enable you to accurately decipher the road through which you are required to ply in order to arrive at that desired end. I would not lie and tell you that it is a game of roses or it is a game for the saints because in reality it isn't.   Life isn't easy is neither should you, do not ever let your guard down, guard your reputation like your life depends on it, you are in charge of your life therefore it is your call that determines where you sway because you are the captain of your own destiny and the master of your own fate. Sometimes, the ones that we refer to as 'saints' know how to get dirty when the need arises (ad trust me =, it will always come every now and then) Now this might piss you off as a believer but I have nothing against people's beliefs as I understand the need to be good but you can be the good guy and not be entirely good or rather let me put it this way, you cannot be the good guy all the time, there are times when you will need to make critical decisions that might be perceived as being bad. I honestly believe that every man has an innate moral compass that sways in the direction of what is actually right; unfortunately, being good is not always the right line of action. I am not saying evil or bad as we like to refer to most actions are okay or trying to undermine the consequences of these actions. What I am doing instead of that is that I am admitting that evil is in the world and that it can serve as a tool even in the hands of men. You will be shocked when you uncover the motive of many "good" people. Think of this for a second, if a person is being good because it makes him /her feel better about himself/herself then it is not as if the person is being good for the sake of it; instead the person is being good for selfish reasons, but then who doesn't have selfish needs and has the urge to solve these urges. Permit me to say that the only guiding rule to your actions should be your conscience and the end result you want to watch unfold in your life. While we all love to lay claim to some sort of moral compass, sometimes you have going to have to look away from certain guiding moral principles and make certain decisions. If the result of your decision is good then it is pardonable to get it under any necessary means, this is what it means for you to be a Machiavellian. The Machiavellian method is one that is very popular in the world of politics and it is very applicable in any area of life that we may find ourselves. My focus in this book will be how you can take over and be dominant in any sector of life you desire to thrive. We cannot all have fortune 5000 companies or all be a part of the Forbes list (as a matter of fact, some people do not want to); if you do not belong to that latter group then it is your duty to get to the top of the business ladder by staying focused, being strong, being powerful, being connected and so on. This book will aim to do two things successfully; First, this book will outline classical Machiavellian statutes that have been the guidebook of global leaders overtime and Secondly, the book will show you how you successfully use these methods of survival to gain unparalleled dominance in the business world;

both objectives will be handled hand in hand and with every passing letter, word, sentence, paragraph and page of the book. You will definitely enjoy each page of the book as there are valuable lessons and ways to getting your desired end. If you don't mind, let me blow your mind away and make you more formidable in the business world all at once.

WHAT WILL MACHIAVELLI DO?

Niccolo Machiavelli (1469-1527) was a civil servant in the Republic of Florence, Italy. Although he was seen majorly as a political philosopher, his thoughts and ideals can be used across all facets of life when it comes to the matters concerning leadership and what leaders should do in order to maintain their positions at the top. Overtime Machiavelli has been and is still being recognized as the father of modern day politics, a posthumous award that the Florentine public servant could never have imagined. In 1513, he authored a book and although the book was not published until 5 years after he died, he died in 1927 by the way. Since its publication, the books cynical approach to power has managed to keep generations glued to THE PRINCE. While a lot of thinkers of his time and even in our times result to impracticality, Mac had several ideas that were not only practical but were also fueled with intellectual accuracy and can be applied in this generation as much as it did in times past. Regarding the morality of leaders, Machiavelli urged them to appear merciful, faithful and religious because it is necessary to appear compassionate no matter how cruel one might be. As George Burns rightly said, "sincerity is everything, if you can fake it, you've got it made".

Some quotes from Machiavelli include;

> 'It would be best to be both loved and feared. But since the two rarely come together, anyone compelled to choose will find greater security in being feared than in being loved"

- "a man who strives after goodness in all his acts is sure to come to ruin, since there are so many men who are not good"
- "The lion cannot protect himself from traps, and the fox cannot defend himself from wolves. One must therefore be a fox to recognize traps, and a lion to frighten wolves"
- "There is no other way to guard yourself against flattery than by making men understand that telling you the truth will not offend you"
- The first method for estimating the intelligence of a ruler is to look at the men he has around him
- Appear as you may wish to be
- A prudent man should always follow in the path trodden by great men and imitate those who are most excellent, so that if he does not attain to their greatness, at any rate he will get some tinge of it.
- It must be considered that there is nothing more difficult to carry out, nor

more doubtful of success, nor more dangerous to handle, than to initiate a new order of things

- ➢ "A prince who has established himself as above, who can command, and is a man of courage, undismayed in adversity, who does not fail in other qualifications, and who, by his resolution and energy, keeps the whole people encouraged - such a one will never find himself deceived in them, and it will be shown that he has laid his foundations well"

- ➢ "Minds are of three kinds: one is capable of thinking for itself; another is able to understand the thinking of others; and a third can neither think for itself nor understand the thinking of others. The first is of the highest excellence, the second is excellent, and the third is worthless."

- "It is essential that in entering a new province you should have the good will of its inhabitants."
- "Therefore the best fortress is to be found in the love of the people, for although you may have fortresses they will not save you if you are hated by the people."
- "Of mankind we may say in general they are fickle, hypocritical, and greedy of gain."
- "That prince who, relying entirely on the people's promises, and has not taken other precautions, is ruined; because friendships obtained by payments, and not by greatness or nobility of mind, may indeed be bought, but they are not owned. In time of need, they cannot be relied upon. Men have less scruple in offending one who they love than one who they fear, for love is preserved by the link of obligation which, owing to the baseness of men, is broken at every opportunity when their self-interest intervenes; but fear

preserves you because a dread of punishment never wanes."

I hope these quotes have given you a tinge of the kind of man that Machiavelli is (I choose to use the present because I believe that there are Machiavelli-like men and women in the world today). He emphasized the importance of power, the importance of perception, the importance of association, the importance of championing change and being a tool to effect change successfully amongst many other lessons to be learnt from him. Throughout the book, we will make attempts to answer the question "what will Machiavelli do?" as we will look at the Machiavellian way of doing things in the business world in a bid to dominate it. Note that Machiavellian ideals were influenced by the harsh realities that bedeviled the political terrain in his time and even though these things are still existent today (in varying degrees); his words therefore should not be misunderstood or taken out of context.

CHAPTER ONE; POWER AND SURVIVAL

For Machiavelli, the protection of your power should be made to be primary and most important if it is taken away then you become useless

Kodak, blackberry, MySpace; all three of these companies were once rulers of their respective sectors and they seemed like they would always dominate. Transform or fade away is a manta that is true because it is what has come to characterize the business world. New ways, new innovations, new ideas and a host of other unique ideas are being discovered or rediscovered from time to time, it is very important to note that as a business owner, you should never try to use old ideas to open new doors.

"The actions of all men, and especially of princes, for which there is no court of appeal, one judges by the result."

To succeed in a business world that continues to change as the second hand on the wall clock, you need to be flexible and be able to blend with the trends that will help you stay conversant and relevant at the same time. It moves like a tornado, the breeze of change, if you do not level up, you will not know when others will leave you behind. Every business leader that wants to stay relevant must learn to move with change and never get left behind by the forces of change. The 'big boys" or the "men" in all industries are the people who have stayed relevant by keeping their eyes on the ground and seeking to find out and always stay abreast with the tides that matter and move the industry. There is no organization that is not concerned; if you refuse to change with the market then you will soon be long gone. Customer service, marketing strategies, core values and so on can through constant evaluation to ensure that they are up to date. As a leader, you needn't be afraid to reinvent and reshape your business to optimize productivity and keep you ahead of the pack. This is easier for you because you know how to do whatever they are doing even better because you have been in the game longer than they can ever imagine.

Machiavelli talks about being a fox in order to find out who the enemies are and that you need to be a lion in order to deal with the parties that want to bring you down. If you fail to act in the case of an imminent threat to you or your business, the end results could be catastrophic and could even lead to the death of that business. There are examples to take cues from. In the history of time, the greatest lesson that there is to learn is that people fail to learn from the misfortunes of others in the past. There are many visible examples of companies that burned to the ground because they could not transform and make the necessary changes, such changes that will cause them to be a force to reckon with. Often times, the ones that don't crumble become shadows of their former selves. For every story of a failed business, there are several other stories of businesses that succeeded because they could stay 'woke'. Looking at the example of Blackberry, the giants when it came to mobile phones and they seemed to be the third wheel in the Apple/Samsung competition. They lost their selling point when they decided to give out the rights to their social networking site. The fact that it existed for Blackberry alone made the social networking more preferred than the likes of Whatsapp and Telegram.

Let's take a timeout to look at a company like National Geographic Channel that has managed to stay relevant in the media sector. What started off as a magazine overtime has now evolved into a media giant and they continue to strive to provide excellent service in television, print, and documentation of the world 130 years later. While similar companies that they started the business with would have folded up today because of changes that happen every time in the business world. National Geographic has managed to reinvent its brand and market it to generation after generation and we all love it! As a business leader looking for domination, it is very important that you embrace transformation, your starting point could be your comfort zone but it doesn't have to be where you will stay.

Growth happens and markets change, therefore, companies must prepare themselves to grow along with these changes. Whether it is in the area of marketing or branding or in any other areas likes recruitment, public relations and so on, The company's culture will need to allow for flexibility in order to ensure that the longevity of such a brand. Excellence is never an option, it should always be a watchword because, with excellence, you can leverage and demand more value. People are willing to part with their hard-earned money if they can feel the value of whatever their money is being spent on. Operational excellence will lead to a 'customer-first' behavior in the company and this will cause them to stay ahead.

It is inevitable for businesses to face disruption in their activities. These disruptions could be as a result of counter activities of government and other regulatory bodies. In the face of such great adversity is the golden opportunity to check company strategies. This will help companies to have a futuristic look. That futuristic look will guide every decision you make as a CEO or as a person in general.

HOW WILLING ARE YOU?

Before I go on to list some business lessons that you can learn from history, let me make something clear, you must be willing to get dirty in the business world if you intend to last long and stay relevant. Getting to the top is very tough and staying there is even a notch tougher. Therefore you should know what your limits are when it comes to how far you are willing to go in order to get a desired end; if I was to urge you, I would urge that you stay limitless because limits are stoppers and they tend to restrict you and put you in a box therefore it is important that you break free from whatever box and pursue your goals with all available resources. Today is all that you are assured of, tomorrow will dance to the tunes of those that set it yesterday therefore it is important that you handle the present (what is real). Work on the present with lessons from the past I order to have a rosy future, this is the simple formula that is needed.

HISTORY AND ITS LESSONS

"A man who is used to acting in one way never changes; he must come to ruin when the times, in changing, no longer are in harmony with his ways"
- Machiavelli

As years become decades and then centuries and so on; the lessons that are available for man to learn from the activities of the people of the past are countless and if you pay attention, you will learn something from history. In the business world, there have been many failures and successes, there have been hostile takeovers and mergers and companies that declared bankruptcy amongst other things. Closely related to these happenings are lessons that can be learnt from history. I will talk about some of these lessons from businessmen in history. They are;

KNOW YOUR MARKET

"Sweat equity is the most valuable equity there is. Know your business and industry better than anyone else in the world. Love what you do or don't do it."
Mark Cuban

In the whole of history, several business owners have thrived because they were able to have a perfect understanding of their market. Knowing several details ranging from the age to the social status and other vital details is important when it comes to dealing with a market. You can be as good as a businessman that you find out the problems that your customers had and even find problems that they did not know. You need to know your market well enough in order to understand how to properly serve them and ensure that they stay loyal to your brand. How can you know your market? It is not rocket science, the knowledge of your target market can be gotten through research, surveys and all other forms of feedbacks. The greatest businesses are those that find the needs of their customers and work hard in order to meet those needs excellently.

FOCUS ON QUALITY

"Quality means doing it right when no one is looking"- Henry Ford

If lessons from the history of the business world are to be followed, then we should always be diligent in the process of creating that product or offering those services. If your brand is known for quality services or products then you will continue to make huge strides in that industry because you have been able to gain the trust of the customers and non-customers alike. Great quality is great for the reputation of your business because it helps your business to be help in high esteem by those that affect the market. Do not be afraid to make investments in exchange for quality. The most expensive commodities in the world today are not just expensive for the sake of it but they are because of the efforts of the manufacturers to make a valuable product. Also, it is very important to test your products severally before sending them out to customers. It is safe to ensure that your products are properly tested to perform maximally before beginning its sale to the general public.

NEVER STOP CREATING VALUE

**"A prudent man should always follow in the path trodden by great men and imitate those who are most excellent, so that if he does not attain to their greatness, at any rate he will get some tinge of it."
Machiavelli**

In order to create value, you must be able to provide your customer with benefits that are at least equal to and in some cases these benefits outweigh the cost. What I have come to discover as trend since time immemorial is the fact that no matter the cost of a commodity, if it has the value that can match the price then there are people that will pay for such a commodity. Therefore as a business owner who wants to get control and then gain power over your industry, you will need to pay attention to value. As long as the value is intact then you don't have to worry about finding demand for your commodity because demand will definitely come for such a valuable product or service.

EFFICIENCY IS KEY

Value alone cannot do the trick; you need to be efficient in the methods that you apply. Doing the right thing every once in a while wouldn't do the trick, you and your team members have to be continually efficient and ensure that you do not willingly break the trust that a customer or a set of customers have bestowed upon you.

"It has been my observation that most people get ahead during the time that others waste." – Henry Ford

I have come to realize that to stay efficient isn't child's play. Being efficient actually means that you will continue to offer value regardless of the situation at hand. Therefore, there is no room for excuses. Once excellence becomes a watchword for you and the members of your team, you will find it easy to be efficient. I agree that hard work is very important, more importantly is working smart. If you work hard and not smart, you are bound to utilize more effort and/or extra time. Working smart has to do with finding the right mix of production cost, pricing and profits for your business.

BEING FIRST IS OVERRATED

This might seem like a contradiction at first glance, but upon much pondering, you would realize that the fact that you are bothered about being first is pointless. The person that is first doesn't have time to bother about those that aren't first, instead of being bothered about who the first is, focus on your own development and work on yourself and your business until you become a force to reckon with. From there it becomes easier to dine with the kings and not just mean men and from dinning with kings, you can attain ultimate power to use in your business. Such a strong network is needed if you are going to dominate the business sphere in whatever industry you may find yourself.

EMBRACE REJECTION...BUT

In reality, there is no need to act like rejection will not always come. What matters most is how we react to it; if you accept the fact that rejection is very possible and even likely in our actions then it will help you because you will always expect it. The fact that you expect it will help you to plan how to handle it if it comes. Most people that later attained greatness; even up till legendary status in life, were once rejected at a point. The rejection helped to motivate them to greater heights. You can choose to get better when you face rejection or you can beat yourself down further; the choice is yours to make.

BE WILLING TO TAKE RISKS

Risks and business should go hand in hand because both work together. As a business owner you should not be afraid to take risky decisions, they are the foundation for greater things in the business world. You have to be ready to calculate your moves to ensure that they are safe moves that will not lead to colossal damage. Before taking any risks, think it through and consider the likely aftermaths of the risks. If the pros are more than the cons then you should go ahead and implement such risks. Once you are able to properly think through the process before finally deciding to take the risks then you can go ahead with it. Whenever you decide to take risks, you are in charge of your thoughts, actions and reactions therefore it is important that you lead by example and show composure and remain optimistic about the risk you took. The difference between the level you are in and the next level is a particular risk that is to be taken. As a business owner you must be willing to think outside the box because that is the more likely way to success. If you take risks and eventually fail at it then you will learn from that mistake and get better with subsequent risks. The best teacher is experience therefore it takes a lot of heart to make certain decisions at certain times under certain circumstances.

CHAPTER TWO: MANAGEMENT

Much than being seen as a process of controlling things and people, management has to do with way more than that. How can you dominate in the world of business? You need to master the act of management because you will need to manage yourself, your team, your enemies, your competition, your thoughts, your decisions and so on. The list of things to manage is endless and more often than not, the difference between those that you see on the front pages of business magazines and those that don't manage to make the cut is the way they manage things and people. In order for you to succeed in anything you do, you will need to have a sense of proper management because that will help you immensely in ensuring success.

Before I go on, I would love to give you an insight about why management is important, and I will do this in terms of the general terms of usage of the word "management". In life generally, there are certain things that all humans have equal measures of them. For starters, every human being has 24 hours in a day, what is different is how we decide to use our time; while some will make god use of each minute they have, others will do little or nothing. Results will always speak for themselves. Like time, there are other things at our disposal that we have to ensure that we use maximally to ensure that we become the best versions of ourselves. The difference between two people could simply be the way they manage their talents, resources, opportunities and so on. In order to make the best use of these opportunities at our disposal, it is important that you manage them and what does it mean to manage these things? It simply means making the best use of them. In managing people also, it is important that you learn the act of management because it will help you bring out the best in people. In life, there is the **potential** and there is the **actuality**. The potential of a person for example is what such a person can achieve when properly managed and the actuality is what that person is able to achieve, your actuality is your reality. In order to become who you are potentially able to become, you must master the act of managing properly. This chapter will endeavor to do justice to the issue of proper management in the business world and we will do this with an end in sight; the domination of the industry that you are in.

Traditionally, management refers to the activities of a person or a group of people involved in the Planning, Organizing, Leading and Coordinating of resources. How can your business make the best use of the resources at its disposal in order to get the best possible results? Answering this question can be a life-long process but once you are able to get a hold of what it takes and how to properly manage things. The roots of the word 'management' can be traced back to Latin to mean 'to lead by hand'. Effective management is done by leading or directing people to do productive and efficient work. How can you manage a business that will dominate the industry that you are in and will cause other companies to step up their game. Here are some tips on how you can successfully get that done;

SET A GOAL AND SEE TO ITS FULFILMENT

It is common for business owners to have short term goals and long term goals, there are certain objectives that you want to see happen for your business in a given time frame. Long term goals are the effects of several short and medium term goals that came to pass. It is important to set goals because they will help in the overall coordination of your business. Your goal is like a destination (however temporal) but then it gives your efforts meaning. If you set a particular goal and you are able to achieve it then you should take out time to acknowledge it and celebrate it with your team. It is very important to cultivate the habit of celebrating your successes as a team because this will not only result in better work relationship. It will also result in more efficiency on the part of your team members that will make the management of the business easier for you and increase productivity.

HAVE THE RIGHT TEAM

I cannot over emphasize this fact. As a matter of fact, this same point could appear in all chapters of the book and I would talk about it differently. Having the right team makes management easier for those at the hem of affairs. If you have a team of passionate, goal-driven, vision-oriented folks at your disposal, I bet you will have no hassle over managing the affairs of members of the team. That brings me to this quick point, it is important that you pay attention to your hiring process, personally I always suggest that you should hire based on referrals because it is important to hire the kind of person that will understand the vision of the business and align it with his/her own. You could have a top product and a very amazing business strategy and still not do great things because of a team that is not up to par. Therefore it is important to spend time to build your team because they determine your company's success or failure.

KEEP YOUR CUSTOMERS HAPPY, YOUR EMPLOYEES TOO!

Regardless of the stage that your company or brand has gotten to, you must never forget this fundamental principle because it will help you focus on other aspects. This is because if you have stable customers that will always come back and be glad to offer referrals then you will recognize the importance of this principle. If you are being honest, you know what the customers in your sector need, but several factors could hinder it. If you have been in a particular industry for at least a year; you should understand how to please customers. If you see companies that are not paying attention to their customer's needs then such companies are bound to fall to the ground.

Human beings are such that if you are able to gain their trust by making them happy with your product, customer service, branding and other things; they tend to forget that other brands exist because you have given them all that they could ask for. What are they asking for? Better customer service, better products, cheaper products and the likes. It is not out of place for a regular customer to ask for better services from you. You will need to find out what the low points are for your company as long as customers are involved. In order to properly treat the customers and gain their trust, you will need to put in consistent work. Do you know certain folks that are so in love with a particular brand that they fail to recognize even the closest alternatives? Keeping your customers happy from time to time and you will have to worry about less in your business.

Keeping the customers happy is one side of a coin and while it will help you maintain sales and give your brand a good image externally, there is another set of people that you have to continually seek and work towards making them happy and they are your employees. Apart from the most loyal ones, most employees will not hesitate to take better offers if they become unhappy on the job. There are certain employees that you just cannot afford to lose (especially when it is to the side of a competitor). Losing an employee is an extreme; but then harboring unhappy employees in your company, is not a wise thing to do. Not only will it reduce the level of productivity in the business, it could also result in friction that could eventually be the death of the business. Why then do you want to take such a huge risk when you can keep your employees happy? Trust me it is easier than you think and maybe one of these days I could write a book about that. The summary of all these is that happy employees and happy customers will keep the management of your business going smoothly, so smooth that the managers will have little or nothing to do.

Customers have the most relevant ideas on how to better run your business, endeavor to always listen to them. It is important to get steady feedback from customers, put a formal approach in place in order to keep listening to customers all the time and acting on their input and making your business bigger.

FIND A MENTOR, BE A MENTOR

Before I tell you why it is important to have a mentor, let me tell you something about the dynamics of the world maybe you will understand how much you can learn from mentors and from being one. Movement in the cycle of life is a continuum that has been since time immemorial, men have always founds ways to solve problems. If you ever imagine the fact that nothing new has been created that wasn't in the world on the first place. Therefore the materials that man is using today for his great exploits have been in existence but they hadn't been discovered in the light with which we know today. Man overtime has had ideas that will help make things easier and overtime these ideas have been passed down from generations. The fact that today we have unlimited access to things through the internet is even a plus. You can be in constant communication with folks from all over the world therefore t makes it easier to learn from people. Think of this, all the ideas that you need to have a successful life are hidden in one book or in the mind of another person. As a person, all you need to do is to find the right sources to connect with and then you can get unlimited access to a world of knowledge. These people will not only provide you with helpful blueprints that will help accelerate you rise to prominence.

The fact that certain people have experienced things that are similar to what you are experiencing (even though it is in a different environment) is a blessing. Think of it, it is like going along an unfamiliar path and then having someone that has gone through the route and knows other people that have too; This person has probably made mistakes that have caused him/her to become wiser. It is important to interact with people who have made it to where you seek to be, it doesn't matter where they made it from. The thing is that the roadmap to success is so wide that you could do 200 different things that will lead to a particular end. Therefore it is important to have mentors that will serve as a source of stability and support; they will be there in your time of need. As important as it is to find mentors, it is also important to have mentees because you can learn a great deal from someone that looks up to you. The act of learning is so amazing that you can learn a whole lot if you look at your life in reverse and your mentee will probably give you a vision of your past while you help them get through it. Don't let pride get in the way of your relationship with either your mentor or your mentee. The greatest people in the business world have had great mentor/mentee relationship. Opera Winfrey was mentored by Maya Angelou; Late Steve Jobs mentored Mark

Zuckerberg while Warren Buffet Mentored Bill gates. These greats seem like they have it all and they do not need mentors; the truth is that we all need mentors at a point in life because there are a lot of things that can be learnt from it.

For mentors

- You must be willing share skills, knowledge and expertise
- Remember that you are role model and act accordingly. Endeavor to show your mentee how it's done and do this with utmost professionalism
- It is important to provide feedback, it is very important to provide feedback in form of constructive criticism and advice on what he/she ought to do.
- Before any mentoring relationship can be said to be successful, the mentor must show interest in the mentoring relationship.
- Celebrate the successes of your mentee.
- Lead by example

- Invest enough time working with your mentee and encourage independent thinking/behavior
- As much as possible, give your honest input to your mentee. Is is necessary to say things as they are.

For mentees

- Make sure you implement your mentor's advice as soon as possible. By doing this, you will encourage such a mentor to offer you more advice.
- Because your mentor's time and opinion is valuable, offer to help him/her with something without asking for anything in return. This will help you create a closer relationship
- Exceed the expectations of your mentor.
- Show gratitude by giving your mentors gifts.

- Build trust with your mentor because mentors can become potential sponsors (when they believe in you)

You should never underestimate the strength of wisdom, especially when it is gotten from experience. In the business world especially, it is necessary to find mentors that will not only help you stand but also show you around. By doing this, they will ensure that you can stand on both feet on your own.

IMPORTANCE OF MANAGEMENT

1) *Accomplishment of your goals*; I said earlier how managing requires you to lay down some goals, these goals are attained through hard work and dedication. Businesses that are making impact in the world today are being managed by management professionals who have managed the business excellently. In

setting goals for a business, it is important to keep employees up to speed with the steps that are being taken ad the goal that is hoped to be achieved. This will help ensure that everyone is on the same page; if the goal can become a collective goal then it becomes a goal that will be gotten with collective effort of a group of like-minded individuals who will put everything in their power to ensure that the goal is accomplished. If you can have a team with these kinds of individuals then you will be sure to attain success. Big companies are companies who always set a goal higher than ever and strive to beat it. With this repeated process, the company grows and with time it becomes a force to reckon with.

2) *Vision and Foresight*: Every business wants to be adequately prepared for the future therefore it is only right for you to have proper vision and foresight to see what your business needs as time passes.

Having a great management will help you have proper plan for the future of your business. Great leaders generally have a clear, positive and compelling vision for the business that guides every step they make and all of their decisions. If you look at a jigsaw puzzle for example, you see the real thing in the beginning before it is later scattered and you then have to use the picture of the complete thing to arrange the incomplete one piece by piece. The final image of the puzzle is the vision that you have for the company. It is what you are working towards every day.

Having foresight is also important in the business world, this is because there are several decisions that you will make because of foresight. With foresight you can also spot threats to your business and handle them accordingly. Without proper management there cannot be a proper goal that the business is striving towards and this could gradually kill the business.

3) *Optimum Utilization of resources*: When there is a good team In charge of the management of a business, such a business will always make the best use of their resources. Through proper planning and adequate organization the management of the company takes away all forms of wastages to the barest minimum. They will also get to achieve efficiency in the day-to-day operation of their business. Also, when resources are properly utilized then it will lead to more worker satisfaction because they will enjoy from the resources at the company's disposal.

4) *Order*: Having a team of managers that know what to do will always help you to keep things in order. Everything about your business will have a standard process of how it is being done. Even the holy

book for the Christians recognizes the importance of order.

APPERANCE IS EVERYTHNG

"Men in general judge more from appearances than from reality. All men have eyes, but few have the gift of penetration"

You are definitely with the phrase "keeping up with appearances", it is important for you to never allow the image of your company to suffer. It is important to guard the image of your company jealously because it is one thing that truly matters. If there is anything that can be done, I mean anything at all to avoid the dragging of your company's public image. The common man is known according to Machiavelli to be impressed by appearance and results; everything in between is not important to man. There are times when you will have to do some "bad" things in order to maintain that appearance. Never beat yourself down for doing the necessary evil; if you do not do it, it might just come back to hurt you and that will likely be deadly.

There are times when folks have gotten life changing jobs, contracts, scholarships and so on because they had the right kind of appearance. Having confidence is another kind of appearance that will always work for you. A confident, well-spoken person will be preferred over one with a better idea but with less confidence and ability to deliver. You have to treat every meeting like it is what will determine your next day on earth. It is important that you are consistent with the image you portray of your business to the world. The world is drawn to images therefore if you know how to create a proper image for your business then you will win the hearts of many people. They will be drawn to you because they will feel a sense of security due to the fact that you are a consistent person or that your brand is consistent.

CHAPTER THREE: WHO ARE YOU AROUND?

"The first method for estimating the intelligence of a ruler is to look at the men he has around him" - Machiavelli

It is important for you to consistently consider the kind of people that are in your corner. Who are the comrades that you can always call on to do get the job done? Who are you around? Do you have the human resources to support the goals you have for your business? Overtime, Machiavelli was able to establish that you are as strong as the people you have around you. You cannot expect to be at the top if you are busy dinning with folks from below. Your network of people around you matters a lot. A great person once said that if as a person/party you need something and the group of people around you (your network) cannot provide it for you then you are not around the right kind of people. It goes without saying that eagles fly together while the other lower birds look from below. It is not a matter of pride but of principles. Machiavelli asserts that if you want to meet a prince (a great person I this terms), you must offer him will get him to be interested in you. It is a rule of life that Machiavelli projected from over 500 years ago and it still works in today's society. Give a sincere evaluation of yourself and check if you are being surrounded by the right type of people, the kind of people that will help you move forward and lend a helping hand if the need arises. This golden rule is important for individuals and much more important for brands. For leaders, it is your duty to make sure that the image of your brand is further strengthened by those who associate themselves with the brand and not otherwise.

It is also important to know the strengths and weaknesses of the people that are under you. Until you are able to recognize the strength of your comrades, you will never be able to maximize their potential. As a businessman that is looking to dominate, there are certain moves that you have to make personally; every other thing can be delegated. When you have groomed the people in your team adequately then you can be assured that they will do amazing things even when you are not there doing constant supervision.

NETWORKING FOR EXCELLENCE

It is important that your business has its "faces", that is, people that represent the company in public events, in business meetings and all other important activities for the company. These people and even other members of your company should be made to understand the importance and the best ways to network for excellence. I will touch on a number of vital points concerning networking.

If you are a business professional wishing to build relationships and grow influence then networking is always a magnificent idea no matter the industry you might be a part of. No matter what industry you're in, networking is always a good idea for business professionals wishing to build relationships and grow their influence. Remember all that networking has to offer the next time you restock your business cards and share them with new connections!

Networking is free most of the time and it is fun because it is filled with like-minded individuals who are all striving towards similar goals. If you go to the right events, you will find people that you can totally work with; people that will be of mutual benefits. Full applause to the internet for making networking way faster and easier but I have to admit that there is nothing comes close to being as good as face-to-face networking and interaction. Networking is so much unlike the workplace because it creates a laid back environment for professionals to meet and help each other. Networking events are organized for professionals where informal chats often lead to the discovery of many opportunities and potential ways through which various people can work together. In the networking process, you are given the opportunity to create a lasting impression in the minds of people that you come across. At the end of the, two things matter; the people you know and the people that know you.

Help, advice and broadening of horizons are just a few perks of networking. Networking can also push you to go further, it can give you certain ideas that you never imagined before. Generally, when networking is done properly, the effect is the expansion of your pool of knowledge. It is important to stay connected to your contacts. Communication is key in strengthening relationships therefore it is important to constantly communicate with the people in your network because that will lead to a window of opportunities like you never imagined. Pick up those business cars and send that email today, make those calls today and you will be glad that you did.

Often times, professionals come up with excuses when it comes to attending such events. You are never too busy to get a break from your computer screen and interact with fellow professionals. Networking events can count as part of work because it is a means to an end which may differ from person to person. There is value in forming and maintaining a strong and diverse contact base what will serve you for years and even decades to come. If you are a startup owner and you are worried about finding communities like that of professionals then you needn't worry about that anymore. There are many startup communities around the world where entrepreneurs share ideas, risks, profits and everything else that there is to share. There are times when there is massive economic uncertainty and these communities have helped and continue to help startups to experience progress during these tough times. For young entrepreneurs, apart from the connections you get from these events, you also get to learn from people that are more experienced than you in the business world.

Networking gives you an opportunity to socialize in a relaxed environment for a few hours. It should be taken seriously and must be done with a plan. It is a process of marketing yourself and your business and gaining the right kinds of connection in the process. I must say that the power of networking is highly underrated. These events are all about creating a platform for the exchange of mutual benefits for both parties. There will be times when you will need insight from someone that can see things from the same angle as you. In your times of need you will be glad that you built a strong network because a man's net worth is only as good as his network.

For most successful people, the key factor to their success story will be the networks that they managed over time. Their interactions with other individuals and their businesses will serve as the nucleus of their networking strategy. There are numerous benefits of networking that are tested and trusted to work over a period of time (with your conscious effort to make it happen). Here is a list of 15 benefits;

1) Having a network will help you to increase your sphere of influence because through people you get to meet other people and that is how the cycle continues for you.

2) You can get opportunities in form of referrals, business opportunities and the likes as a result of the network of people that you have around you.

3) In the business world it is important that you are in a position where you can be more visible. Your visibility level has a lot of influence on how far you will go. Networking will help you gain access to more people and raise your profile.

4) A lot of folks gain momentum by being around the kind of energy that you get while networking. The people in business that network are those that are really going for it and they can serve as great influences on you.

5) Having a network makes it easy to get assistance concerning issues you might have, support for ideas that you might have and advice on a wide range of matters. It will help you have people in your close circle that can offer valuable help to you in the pursuit of your own dreams.

6) Also, having a network gives you the opportunity to help those that might be in need of help in your network. It is important that you help people when they need it because not only is it right to do so, but also because they are several hidden benefits of being good to others in their times of need.

7) Having a network is also very important because your network serves as a means of getting credible information for you and this is a priceless asset in the business world

8) Networking events serve as an opportunity for bright minds to show

their knowledge and subsequently use it as a bargaining chip. The exchange of ideas is one common denominator in networking events they could be dinners, luncheons, retreats, conferences and a host of other things.

9) If you seek to get brand new insights and other perspectives or ways of doing things in your industry, then you need to attend networking events.

10) Networking events can be really helpful for people that lack confidence, it increases confidence. In networking events, you are made to push yourself to connect and talk with new people whether you like it or not.

11) Events meant for networking are great points of meeting for future business partners, suppliers, staff or friend.

12) By networking, you will get to know about products and services that you would not have otherwise heard of. Asides this fact, networking helps you to stay

abreast with all that is happening in your industry. There is a huge chance that you are plagued by (almost) the same kind of problems with the people in your network. You can get the solution to some of your toughest problems from discussing with a fellow professional like yourself.

13) Networking events can also serve as a way to bounce ideas around a wide range of connections. You will get numerous outlooks on the idea and it will help you to better understand the idea and make it into a far better plan than you initially had.

14) You should always look forward to networking events because they serve as means of marketing for not just your business but for yourself as a person.

15) Connections are everything and they are strengthened by having a strong network around you.

Make sure to attend networking events because it has hefty benefits that come at little or no price.

"Since love and fear can hardly exist together, if we must choose between them, it is far safer to be feared than loved"

Let us take a break from the business world for a minute and learn a life lesson from Machiavelli and this part is one that I really find to be interesting. If you are supposed to choose, what will your choice be? Both have virtually the same effect on you, the difference between both lies in the reason why the person adores you, could be out of love or out of fear. I would take my time to explain.

It is way safer to be feared than to be loved, whether by your peers or by other companies. Having both is the ideal but in cases where it is impossible to have both then by all means you should rather be feared than loved. Fear is strengthened by the dread of punishment which is always effective while the bond of love can be easily broken when men feel like it will be to their advantage.

Fear is a more reliable foundation that you can build your power on. Men will always look for their own advantage when it comes to his dealing with others. Therefore those that you love can switch up on you; love is something that can stop when the person feels like it. On the other hand, a person that fears you will always fear you unless you decide to switch up on your own. A lot of people mistake the need for control as being selfish when it is actually what most humans want. Life is better when you are in control of most of your circumstances; man is said to be in control of circumstances. If it is the case that man is in charge of circumstances then it only makes sense for you to master how to control men because by doing that you will be in control of most events that affect your life.

CHAPTER FOUR: USE AND GET USED (to it)

This topic might seem a little sensitive and most people will probably avoid it hypocritically. And we are going to be truthful, we would agree that it is a use and get used world; since it is a reality, why try to talk against it or avoid getting to talk about it in the first place? The truth remains that everyone that is in the world right now is either being used or using someone; as a matter of fact we all use people both knowingly and unknowingly. The truth remains that man isn't made to stay alone therefore it is important to accept the fact that everyone uses people to his or her advantage. Humans can be tools to certain ends at times and you need to learn how to deal with humans because it is a necessity especially in the business world. I have tried to establish that usage of humans isn't always necessarily evil and that it is a necessity in our world. Since it is necessary to use people in the course of our life, I think it is only fair to perfectly understand how it works in order to avoid being on the defensive.

There are about 7 billion people in the world today and everyone has some goal that he/she is chasing after. The world is such that humans can strive to become what they wish to be and in doing this, there will need to be a degree of cooperation here and there. Think of the effects of your single actions on people or better still, imagine how many people every action you make (especially in business) will affect. The truth is that you can either choose to have an effect on people or be affected by people, either ways you are being used or using people. From time to time you must have helped someone in achieving a dream that is entirely theirs, that is just how life is. I have below shed some light on how to effectively use people in achieving your goals;

1) APPEAR VIRTUOUS; everyone loves the guy with virtue, the person that they feel like they can trust, the kind of person that they may describe as being "good". This is

not a book where I get to dictate moral standards to you but it is important to appear that way even if it is not your true nature. You must also know how to appear compassionate, moral and devout.

REWARD AND PUNISHMENT: These are tools that have to be used correctly in order for you master the act of properly using people. Both are incentives that will definitely yield magnificent results in people. It is very important to reward results because it serves as a promise for great work and oftentimes it works well. It is also very important to punish wrongdoings whenever you notice it in people. If you notice wrongdoings and you refuse to curb it through punishment then it is bound to get worse. Master the art of correctly dishing out rewards and punishment and you will have mastered more than 40% of the skills needed in the usage of humans to get to your goals.

    2) RECOGNIZE LOYALTY; in using people, you will find people that either genuinely

cares about you or they seem like they do. One thing you must never forget it that no one is to be trusted; on the other hand there are certain people that will always look out for you. Loyalty is rare but it is not totally impossible therefore when found, it should be guarded jealously. Treat the loyal ones the best way possible because loyalty is a choice that only the brave at heart can commit to.

3) INFLUENCE; the power of influence has to be something that you recognize and use effectively in your dealings with humans. One thing that most people fail to tell you is that you could have the best network in the world and fail to make the best out of it. What matters more than the people you know is how much of an influence you are to them. More often than not, influence is a natural thing but you can develop yourself into a person that has influence on people.

I want to briefly talk about what I call the separation principle, what does it mean? The separation principle means that you are eliminating the unimportant things to focus on that which is important to you. There has to be separation for order to exist. All the principles I have given you for success in the business world will only be tools except they are used in the right way. As a person, you must learn to separate work affairs from your family matters, you must be able to separate the good and the bad and so on. It is important to make clear distinctions to aspects of your life. This separation of various aspects of your life is necessitated by the need to coordinate your life orderly.

You also need to be able to separate the good from the bad times and move on regardless. I once heard that what matters more than the things that happen to us is our response; the way you respond to the events in your life will go a long way in determining how far you go in the business world. Recognizing that there are good and bad situations will help you to respond to events accordingly and your response might just be what will save your company from a major setback.

CHAPTER FIVE: POWER

Machiavelli emphasized the importance of power; once power is lost then man is nothing. Power is needed in all aspects of life from politics to religion to education and other facets. The business world is one place where you need power in order to gain the attention of those that matter. The dynamics of power according to Machiavelli can be said to be brutish and filled with violence, it is mainly because he referred to mostly matters in politics. Power in the business world is less brutish and more economical and to play the dirty games that people play, you must recognize the rules to the game. There are certain types of powers in business, it is best that you combine a couple of them depending on what you need the power for. Most times, power gets into people heads and they begin to make wrong decisions, this should not be you because it never ends well. Typically there are 5types of power;

1) COERCIVE POWER; this is when a person's style of leadership is by threats and force. This type of person will be seen as being too forceful and will likely lose the respect of his employees. Sometimes it is necessary to use this type of power but when a person employs this as the only kind of power then there is a problem. **"Never attempt to win by force what can be won by deception"-Machiavelli**

2) LEGITIMATE POWER; this is the power gotten by being at a higher position. It is the kind of power that you have over the people under you in the chain of command. This power should never be abused because it can be easily taken away in the instance of abuse. This type of power is not gotten in a rush; it is gotten through time and time of hard work and being on your craft. This kind of power is a continuum therefore it is important that you do not get complacent and feel like

you have gotten to the peak. People at the peak are still striving to remain there therefore it is never the right time to stop growing.

3) **REFERENT POWER; this kind of power is not common but it is one of the most efficient forms of power because you do not need to use force. This kind of power is owned by people who are charismatic and can appear to have positive values. This power is the most valuable kind because people are willing to do things for you because of certain admirable qualities that you possess.**

4) EXPERT POWER; this kind of power is gotten through a leader's experience and skills. As an expert, you are in the position to use your expertise and other necessary skills that you must have gathered over time to help employees with whatever

difficulties that they might be facing. This kind of power is helpful and can only be gotten through hard work. The good thing about this kind of power is that you can always find people that will value it.

5) REWARD POWER; this kind of power is gained by a person's ability to reward good work. A leader that uses this style in order to encourage the people under him to do great work. The reward power is very positive but it lacks real substance because if people only work hard because of the rewards; there is a huge tendency that they will stop as soon as the rewards stop.

SECRECY AND POWER

Oysters open completely when the moon is full; and when the crab sees one, it throws a piece of stone or seaweed into it and the oyster cannot close again so that it serves the crab for meat. Such is the fate of him who opens his mouth too much and thereby puts himself at the mercy of the listener." **Leonardo Da Vinci (1452-1519).**

Warren Buffet, J.K Rowling, Albert Einstein, Charles Darwin and a host of other notable men and women in the history of the world all agree on one thing, they are all introverts. This is not an appeal or some sort of attempt to convince you to become an introvert, on the other hand I am trying to point out to you that great men know how to keep quiet and let their actions speak. Often times, the greatest people are the ones with the fewest words. If you plan to dominate the business world in whatever industry you find yourself then you must master the act of bridling your tongue. The world as we have it is a very noisy one, every corner that you turn to you hear sounds from cars, music, people and so on. In a world where silence is almost non-existent, it is important that you try to drown the noise and just learn, silently. There is a kind of correspondence between power and secrecy or the art of being silent. There are reasons why I think it is important to be silent because power lies in there;

"Power is in many ways a game of appearances, and when you say less than necessary, you inevitably appear greater and more powerful than you are"- Robert Greene.

Silence helps you to destabilize a speaker because humans are programmed to expect words from you and it is amazing that most humans cannot resist silence. When you are silent, humans would become uncomfortable because they will need to analyze you by your words. When you do not speak then you do not give out unnecessary information in the process of communicating.

Silence can be a tool of empowerment if used wisely; when you are silent then you are able to analyze the speaker and then this gives you the power of the listener. When people talk too much it could mean that they are trying to justify themselves and this ultimately causes them to appear weak. Powerful people have experts that speak on their behalf at major meetings. The less you talk; the deeper and more powerful you would seem.

Another important reason why silence and secrecy is important is because it forces you to focus on body language. It is important to master body language to a certain extent if you are going to take control of the business world. While most humans can make attempts to bridle their tongue, only a few can pay attention to their body language. Once you are able to correctly read people's body language effectively then it will be a weapon that you can use for a lifetime. Not only will you be able to communicate in silence with other experts in a 'higher' language. Non-verbal communication techniques are very important and if you can take time off to master it, you will be better off. Powerful people are not necessarily the best speakers, they often do not speak that much but they have mastered the art of non-verbal communication; you should too!

In the world today, people have a special kind of love or respect for great listeners. Being a great listener pushes the speaker to fill the void and keep talking, this way you will get access to information. The more a person talks, the more he runs at the risk of exposing too much information which will eventually be to your advantage. It is better to look stupid than to open your mouth and clear all doubts. Say less than what is necessary at all points.

Silence, can also be used a means of drawing attention to yourself in the middle of an important speech. Silence in-between words give your words more clarity and cause people to pay more attention to you.

"The right word may be effective, but no word was ever as effective as a rightly timed pause" – Mark Twain

Silence is a very powerful tool and Powerful people and good negotiators have mastered the art of silence. Speaking too much is never attractive and most times it just further shows a person's weaknesses. Therefore it is important to learn when to speak and when to be quiet because silence helps you to keep power.

CHAPTER SIX: IT IS A GAME, PLAY THE HELL OUT OF IT

"I'm not interested in preserving the status quo; I want to overthrow it"- Machiavelli

Personally, I believe that life should be lived with one guiding rule, the rule that there are no options beyond reach. In trying to get your biggest dreams to become real, sometimes it becomes necessary that you go to certain extremes.

"Never was anything great achieved without danger" – Machiavelli

This is not a way to encourage the evil tendencies that you might have, instead it is to tell you that you are more than capable of doing the things that you dream of doing as a young man/woman in the business world. Although, this game is not fair, the fact that life itself is not fair makes everything acceptable in the pursuit of these things. We are all players who constantly seek to outshine others for whatever reasons that we have. The competition in the business world makes everything even more interesting. We are all trying to lift the flags of our respective teams while trying to make an impact at the same time. It is important to recognize the importance of teamwork and use it to your advantage at every point in time. How can you maximize the potentials that you have? This has to be the main question that you will ask from time to time. I will give you some tips that I know will be of immense help for you in your everyday dealings with people in the business world.

If we look at the world of business today, you will notice several trends and several people making moves; ensure that you do not get lost in the sauce. It is easy to get distracted in the midst of the madness; do not forget to remain yourself and never forget the true essence of things. Man's greed is one reason why he will always strive to get more than what he will ever need in life; while greed could be a good incentive sometimes, it is not always one and it could lead to turmoil. Earlier I used the saying that the end justifies the means and this should be your whole life mantra. You should be able to define your own terms of success and do what you have to do to get it.

Being the good guy is one thing that has been overplayed and it has become overrated. If we are being honest, there are no such things as good guys or bad guys in the business world (or in the world in general). It is a matter of who gets caught doing the bad things. Personally I do not think that there are good or bad people; instead there are people that do good and bad things depending on the expected outcome. There are times when the game could get ugly, learn to use the principle of separation to ensure that you get yourself back in the game.

Never be hesitant to call a timeout and spend some time on the sidelines studying the game. It is normal to almost get lost in the process of chasing dreams, make sure you have clearly defined goals and let them guide your every move. The fact that the business world is one big game makes it important for you to have a strategy that will guide you. A man without a set of rules which he follows will only take a while before he self-destructs. No matter the level that you are on, it is important to have principles and strategies that will guide your every move. It is important to consider moves before making them because sometimes one wrong move can spell doom for you. Another thing to note is that mistakes are bound to happen therefore do not stay sobering over past mistakes, learn to live in the now. It makes no sense to worry over how you ought to be living and in the process ignore what you are supposed to be doing. The game is not for the faint-hearted or the thin skinned because those kinds of people will get thrown away when turbulent winds arise.

Survival tips in the business world

As promised, I have decided to share 16 tips that will help your survival in the business world. These tips will be helpful whether you own your business or you are working under someone else.

1) Hope for the best and expect the worst, why? In life as well as in the business world, expectations hurt and therefore it is better to expect the worst. If you go on hoping for something and expecting it at all means, you might just be in for a disappointing discovery. Work hard with all the means at your disposal but then never hurt yourself by expecting too much.

2) In order to survive in the business world you have to make plans that will guide your every move. Business plans are a must in every business because most businesses will fail without a proper plan in place. When you make it and habit to always make plans, you would realize how orderly is going to become.

3) In sports, players are always familiar with the standings and other vital pieces of information. This same rule applies to the business world too; it is important that you monitor the market from time to time. This will help you have a better understanding of the market and eventually help you in making smart business decisions.

4) Time management is one habit that you will have to cultivate if you are going to get to the top of the business world. Treat lateness like a plague; treat deadlines like your life depends on it. Make it a habit to properly manage your time and you will be amazed with how much ease you will have in your life.

5) Solitude is very dangerous in the business world and i would advise against it. Being alone is dangerous therefore it is important that you find people that are going towards the same direction and be friends with them.

6) Seek fulfillment and not just a large bank account; people often get to a point in their career when they do not feel any drive or motivation. This could be as a result of a lack of fulfillment on their part. It is important to make loads of money and to yield influence but more importantly, seek fulfillment along with these things.

7) Make it a habit to celebrate your successes. Often times when we are going through tough times we tend to forget that we are capable of doing really amazing things. Also, it is important to celebrate hard-work, reward yourself with a gift or with a getaway. Do something unusual when you attain new heights.

8) The best thing that you can do for yourself is to have faith in yourself. It is amazing that you can achieve a whole lot of things if and only if you have faith in yourself. Having faith in oneself will give

you enough boosts to chase that which you truly desire until you achieve it.

9) This tip is one that people do not always pay attention to and it has to do with being a professional in anything that you find doing. If you have a reputation for treating things professionally then it gradually becomes a habit and this is one habit that is truly rewarding.

10) Never stop learning, there is always something new to learn. The brightest minds in the world today have a habit of constantly wanting to learn. If you are someone who is always ready to learn then people will love to work with you because you will be teachable.

11) Recognize that change is a constant and be ready to change. Flexibility is one important attribute that anyone can have in the business world. Trends come and go but trendsetters remain, it is important to learn how to dance to the tunes regardless of how often they change. By

doing this, you are certainly going to be around for a long time.

12) As important as it is to get 6 figures and to achieve all other goals that you might have set for yourself, it is very important to pay attention to your health because you can only perform as your maximum potential when you are in good health. Check yourself regularly and always ensure that you get rest as often as you can.

13) It is important to work hard but it is more important to work smart in order to achieve more than the average hard worker. There are tools at your disposal to make it easy to do tasks easily and efficiently, use these tools wisely and stay ahead of your game.

14) The importance of the internet as the ultimate PR tool cannot be over-emphasized; as a matter of fact the key players in the game have come to recognize the immense benefits of using

the internet (especially social media) as a viable tool in order to reach your desired audience. The way you relate with the public through your business goes a long way to shape the way your company is perceived.

15) Fail forward! What does this mean? It simply means that whenever you fail, look at the place where you fell for the sake of learning from it and from there look forward. By doing this, it becomes impossible for you to make the same mistake twice because you will keep learning from the past and it will serve as a clear blueprint for your future endeavors.

16) Lastly, it is important to enjoy the process of business and learn from it. Just like life itself there are a lot of experiences that you will go through that will make you a better person. If this is the path you have chosen then you will live the rest of your life (or most parts of it) experiencing the

business world. It is easy to get into the process and not enjoy it but its best to get into the process and enjoy the hell out of it!

CONCLUSION

"Everyone who wants to know what will happen ought to examine what has happened: everything in this world in any epoch has their replicas in antiquity"- MACHIAVELLI

The world today is a reflection of the things that happened in times past and we are all reliving the history of the world. This means that we have a manual for virtually everything we do; one is tempted to ask why we still make mistakes? Is there any way which we can totally avoid mistakes? Yes, the best and only way to avoid mistakes is by not trying anything new. If you are involved in a new process that you are not familiar with, it is normal for you to make mistakes. The only time that you should dislike mistakes is when they become repeated; at that point they become decisions and are no longer mistakes. I would start by telling you that it is okay to make mistakes, what is not okay is making the same mistake more than once. Mistakes are meant to show us samples of what we should avoid in the constant pursuit of dreams.

Passion, a lot of people work in industries that they do not enjoy being in and constantly live through the frustration. This is nothing short of slavery and this is not what anyone should get into. It is not enough to want to get into the business world because of the appearance, anyone can look good in a suit and tie; the question remains if your passion and your reality are the same, If not then it is a waste. Doing something that is in line with your passion is a great way to live.

Once you are able to discover where you passion lies then the next step is to focus on that passion. What does it mean to focus? Focus just means finding what you love to do best and doing it consistently. If you take a look at professionals, it is easy to fall in love with who they have become overtime. One thing that our society is failing to recognize is the importance of being in the process of learning. Today's professionals are amateurs that did not give up yesterday. These days, people wish to start from the top or somewhere close to it forgetting that it takes a lot of work to get to the top. It would take a lot of sacrifice from you if you decide to thread that part. Greatness is not some sort of experience that some people were destined to face, it is something that we are all given the permission to chase and only those who can consistently chase will eventually get there. Let me remind you that greatness is not something that you just wake up to discover that it has been bestowed upon you. No one will bestow greatness upon you, you have to be willing to work for whatever you desire. Very often, people think of the immediate and that is alright, those are not the kind of people that this book is meant for. This book is meant for people who can chase a dream no matter what it takes. Such a dream could take months, years or even a lifetime to fulfill. The ride to greatness is mostly a long one and this is why it is very important that you find that which will motivate you and drive you to do the amazing things in your life.

I touched on the issue of time-management earlier, it is important for you to discover/find/reinvent yourself. This has to be done in order to find where your passion lies. Once you discover that which you have a passion for then you should endeavor to focus completely on it. There is no point multi-tasking because this means that your focus is divided; focus on one thing and keep doing it until you arrive at greatness. There should never be a time in your life when you stop having goals for yourself because creating these goals will give you something that you are working towards and hence you will put maximal efforts into making sure that such a goal becomes reality.

Another reason why it is important to clearly state what your goals are and focus on achieving them is that there are a lot of distractions in the world today. More than ever, there are several ways to spend your time relaxing or having fun. One thing that I have come to discover is that comfort is the enemy of growth. You are not likely to experience growth when you are in your comfort zone, it is important to come out the confines of your comfort zone and get involved in the real world of uncertainty and hope for the best. If you are able to ignore the distractions by keeping your eyes on the price, you will definitely arrive at greatness. It is only a matter of time before you arrive at those golden gates of greatness.

Like Machiavelli, I believe that there is some degree of luck in the affairs of great men and this luck or 'fortuna' as it is referred to in Italia. Luck in itself is nothing, for luck to affect you then you must be in a position where you can apply luck. Therefore if you decide not to put in the work then even when you get lucky you would probably not know what to do. It is also important that you recognize that growth is a process (mostly gradual) therefore it is important that you do not despise the level that you are in right now because it is going to be a part of the process of getting you ready for greatness. The most important factor is growth, as long as you are committed to the process of growing yourself and learning from your mistakes then your climb to the top is almost certain.

Everyone has dreams but not all dreams become goals, the difference between dreams and goals is the work that is put into making that dream into reality. This is what differentiates the successful people from the unsuccessful ones. Another thing that separates them is the fact that successful businessmen know that they should find answers to certain important questions that gives them a clue on how to build the impact of the business. Questions like 'How do I generate ideas?' 'How do I solve problems?' Finding real answers to these questions will go a long way in helping you to build a successful business venture.

In life we have an array of choices to make in order to live the best possible life as we deem fit. Our choices, conscious decisions, actions, hopes and aspirations in pursuit of our dreams are nothing but a sigh of strength, hope, faith and confidence in ourselves. All through this book, I have given helpful information that will help you immensely in your bid to dominate the business world. Knowing these things is just a part of the whole process; more importantly is the application of these things in your everyday life. Oftentimes, we hear things like "easy does it" and the likes; if you are looking for the easy way out then it is safe to stay idle.

Get real, get away from your ideas and the plan that you have created in your head or on paper and actualize the plan. Remember to begin where you are, it all begins with a decision to do this to the best of your ability. If it were easy, there will be millions of billionaires in the world today. Greatness is that differentiating factor that I spoke about at the start of the book.

Therefore by all means necessary, pursue greatness! Cheers!

www.ingramcontent.com/pod-product-compliance
Lightning Source LLC
Chambersburg PA
CBHW051757250726

48659CB00001B/463